W9-BFZ-876

CALIF·150·2000·RNIA

THROUGH AN ARTIST'S EYE

In Celebration of the

150th Anniversary of California Statehood

in the Year 2000

Steve Simon

CALIFORNIA

THROUGH AN ARTIST'S EYE

FEATURING THE FINE ART & VERSE OF

Steve Simon

SIMON FINE ART
BALBOA ISLAND, CALIFORNIA

www.stevesimon.com

This book is dedicated to all who have preserved and protected California's natural environment and to all those who appreciate the sublime and soulful enrichment found in her treasure trove.

Special thanks to friends Tom & Arabelle Brown for your loyal support.

Published by:

Simon Fine Art
P.O. Box 34
Balboa Island, CA 92662

tel: (949)723-1100
www.stevesimon.com

ISBN 0-9652771-3-5

©Steven Simon, Jr., 1999
All rights reserved. No part of this
book may be reproduced in any format,
whether printed or digital, without prior
and written consent of the author.

Associate Producer • Jeff Mikolajczak
Edited by • Donna St. Jean Conti

Manufactured in China by Imago

TABLE OF CONTENTS

Sometime in 1997, I learned that California would soon be celebrating a milestone anniversary during a very special year. It would celebrate 150 years of statehood in the year 2000. "A sesquicentennial celebration at the turn of the millennium" seemed more than a mouthful, it seemed the perfect reason for a landscape artist to indulge in the beauty of this extraordinary state.

So I set out to portray her beauty through my own eyes. I chose to attempt this task through the mediums of oil painting and verse. In tandem, I hoped, the two art forms would offer the latitude to express what images or words alone could not.

Early in 1998 the odyssey began. Knowing very little about this enormous state and having never seen her for myself was initially rather imposing. As I embarked on the journey, however, being unacquainted paradoxically proved to be a great advantage rather than the impediment I had feared it would be. Traveling to these sites as virgin experiences fueled creative fires I do not think I would have found had the beauty of these places been otherwise common to me. My wanderlust would anxiously await the next excursion and embark on it with great suspense. A wide-eyed childlike wonder left behind years ago seemed to find a reprise. These experiences inspired the first chapter entitled *Childlike Wonder*.

The joy I found in observing and painting California's amazingly diverse landscape had a tempering effect on daily stress as well. When presented with the enormity and beauty of this state, I realized how relatively silly and insignificant my daily worries really were. This is not to say we do not each have an important purpose or roll which we must take seriously, quite the contrary. Discovering a sense of purpose and enjoying the beauty in things frees us from lending too much weight to otherwise insignificant tribulations. Chapter 2—*On The Lighter Side*—presents this theme.

Prior to beginning my travels, I knew I would be in for a treat, but the extraordinary variety of beautiful things to see in California surpassed even my loftiest expectations. Surprises occurred in dramatically inspirational fashion. California is awash in the magnificent, the superlative. Beyond the calming effect of easing my daily woes, these experiences also seemed to breathe life into my very spirit. Through these experiences I gained for nature a deeper sense of *Reverence, Gratitude and Respect*—the third chapter.

Still more inspirational, however, were the messages nature herself seemed to be offering. Sometimes these messages were bold and loud, other times subtle, but always there for the open, third eye to see. These were collected in the fourth chapter—*Absorbing Her Lessons*.

One cannot help but feel a spiritual enrichment from such closeness with nature. This kinship between man and the elements enriches our soul. The fifth chapter—*Discovering Silence, Dreaming and Believing*—chronicles the nexus between nature's peace inducing rhythms, our own soulful dreams, and the essence of faith.

The final chapter—*Queen Califia Concludes*—assimilates the themes of each of the preceding chapters. California's 150th anniversary of statehood and her illustrious history are celebrated while an eye toward the future is cast on the collective opportunity of the next millennium.

Perhaps as you explore the California between these covers, you may feel the same quickening I feel to explore, learn from, and be inspired by her. Above all, I hope you enjoy the journey as much as I have.

Happy Sesquicentennial, California!

Chapter 1

Childlike Wonder

Niguel Shores - South Orange County
oil on canvas, 16 x 20 inches

California

A little girl came from far away.
She heard much of this great state.
She implored her teacher—master, she preferred to call him—
"Tell me all about it!"

The teacher spoke proudly of his native soil:
  In this Golden State you shall see magnificent things.
  You shall see . . .
    Not just coastline, the majestic Big Sur
    Not just desert, the unforgiving Death Valley
    Not just mountains, the awesome Sierra Nevada
    Not just farmland, the fertile Central Valley
    Not just trees, the mighty Sequoias.

The student replied:
  Master, I cannot wait to see these for myself!
  Where I come from . . .
    We do not have such wonderful things.
    I have even marveled at the beauty of a single flower,
    Stood in awe of the bird in flight.
    You have these here, too, don't you?

He smiled affirmatively at his new prodigy and spoke no more.

Laguna Beach
oil on canvas, 24 x 12 inches

othing but Net

This is what sand lot basketball really means

Your mind wandering to childhood dreams

What a great world it used to be

Loyal fans swarmed to come see me

Winning shots hit nothing but net

Now, age does fantasies neglect

Mature goals and occupation

Age, why steal imagination?

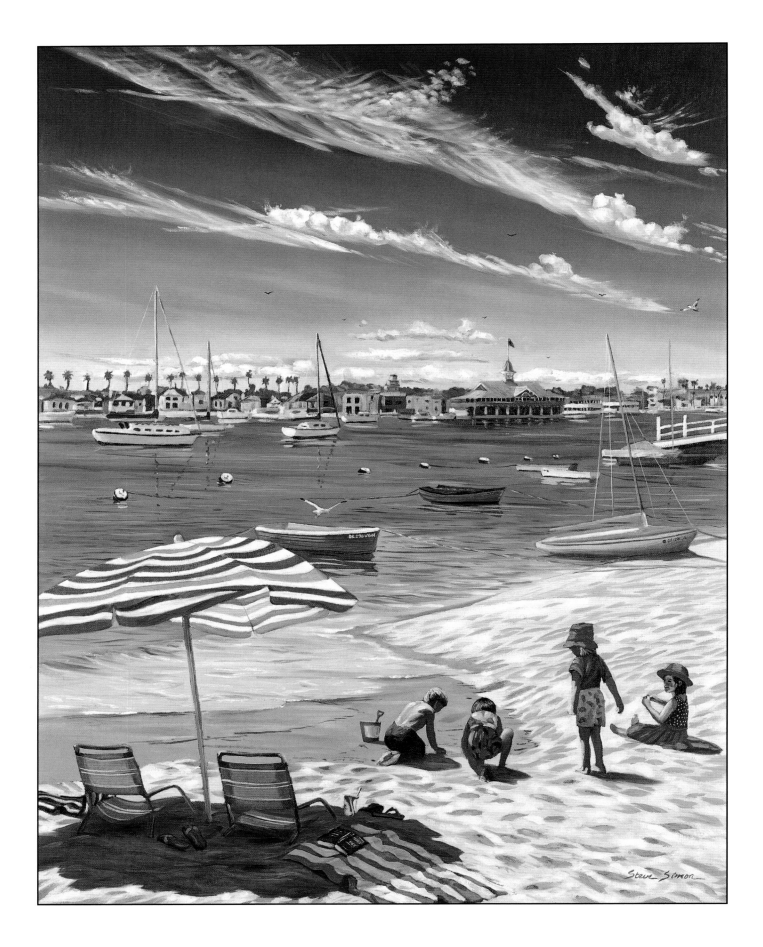

Balboa Island - Newport Beach
oil on canvas, 22 x 28 inches

hore Chores

On wet sand along the shore

They plot out the afternoon's chore

Without reward or outside motivation

Self-assured, locked in concentration

No quest or urgent goal in mind

Their ambition is of a different kind

The pleasure of this simple activity

Engrossed in their own creativity

When Trees Dance

Spring arrives with clockwork determination

Winter's freeze thaws with brilliant animation

River betrayed by its otherwise sleek glide

Loses its bottom and goes for a joy ride

Exploding into a thunderous cool mist

A playground is created difficult to resist

The mist revives the trees down below

Who in their joy put on their own show

This can be the only logical explanation

How trees, like children, danced in jubilation

Bridalveil Fall - Yosemite National Park
oil on canvas, 18 x 36 inches

Joshua Tree National Park
oil on canvas, 36 x 18 inches

 he Curious

Neither the leaves which change color and fall to the ground

Nor needles evergreen or the fans of a palm

Not the wood of a tree or its hearty bark

Nor the flesh of a cactus or its spines so sharp

Like Joshua's welcoming arms before the Promised Land

Threatening, just the same, like a looming ambush at hand

Captivatingly beautiful, yet beastly and haunting

Humorously appealing, yet eerie and daunting

Beholding, I recall the curiosity of being a child

When everything was new and intriguingly wild

Julia Pfeiffer Burns State Beach - Big Sur
oil on canvas, 30 x 40 inches

reedom Child

Free, free, meandering the kingly coastline
Hitching a ride on a sun's mellow departure
Bidding farewell to another paradisiacal day
Balancing a cold, blackening sea with a warm, painterly sky

Free, free, tickling the boughs of the content pines
Mounting up with the raptor above his dominion
Calling his shrill wail over this land
Exalting from high in powerful, graceful liberty

Free, free, diving the kelp forests
Gliding with a sea otter on a curious journey
Playing his game immersed in aquatic therapy
Entertained by the unusual and bemused with the mundane

Free, free, marshaling the strength of steadfast cliffs
Teaming together against the relentless surf
Dusting away the fog with a pampas grass plume
Allowing Nature to hold me like the child of Her womb

Ah, this is the land my child has come to see
Free
Free is the child in me!

Chapter 2

On the Lighter Side

Santa Catalina Island
oil on canvas, 36 x 24 inches

Catalina Dreamin'

From the mainland, dolphins escort our ferry ride

As if sent by the island to swim starboard and port side

We arrive at a harbor snug and cozy

Island pace gentle and downright dozy

Commotion back home but a memory distant

Feels so good relishing the present instant

Oh, to trade it all in, never go back

Hang out here in an old, island shack

Sailboat's Ballad

Slow your pace, forget the clock

Rescue me from this rickety dock

Untie my ropes, untether your soul

Trust in the wind to take control

Fill my sails with life-giving breath

Let's celebrate the beautiful sunset

Santa Barbara Marina
oil on canvas, 24 x 36 inches

San Diego Harbor
oil on canvas, 36 x 24 inches

The Schooner and the Skyline

A schooner moored with dinghy in tow

Perfect solace for the city slicker on the go

It's quitting time Friday, he disrobes the power tie

Shuns rush hour and watches land lubbers scurry by

Where's everyone going with such breakneck pace?

The paradoxical hurry to leave the workday rat race

On board, the executive-turned-captain unwinds and relaxes

Forgetting today's meetings, phone calls, and faxes

Though still in eye shot of his corner office suite

The skyline view is difficult to beat

So he begins to strategize with a little imagination

How to one day make the schooner his new office location

ongboarder's Bravado

Come on, let's take the day off, head out of town

Load up your "Woody" and wax 'em down

I'll meet you at our nostalgic gathering spot

"The Point" of course, in case you forgot

I'll bet my "Microbus" I can still hang ten

On my favorite board and loyal ole friend

And if some annoying, young rats try to spoil our day

We'll show 'em how it's done the old-fashioned way

The Point, San Onofre
oil on canvas, 48 x 24 inches

Santa Monica
oil on canvas, 24 x 30 inches

anderlust

On an urban path well-paved

Or a wilderness trail self-blazed

Under a sun midday strong

Or amidst shadows growing long

In search of intriguing new places

Or the pleasure of meeting new faces

To experience other cultures and discover new ways

This is how I wish to pass the rest of my days

Why not just pack up and head out with my girl

Take my well-healed shoes and wander this world

White Out

Driving along on a winter business trip

A blinding blizzard suddenly let rip

Why does this always happen to me?

I've got places to go, people to see

As a young boy, nothing made me cheer up

Like buttermilk pancakes with heaps of syrup

So, I set out like a young, silly child

To eat a full stack, generously piled

Exiting the highway, I found a greasy spoon

My luscious prize couldn't arrive too soon

Eating, I reminisced how much it used to please

When school would close on days like these

I closed my eyes and imagined a setting

Where snow like this wouldn't be so upsetting

In my daydream I could see a wooden bridge

Pine trees scattered on a steep mountain ridge

Chilly, black water and white, powdery snow

Balanced with a sky in warm, sunny glow

A vision so captivating it made me reason

Heaven, too, must have a winter season

When reality set in I began to understand

For every blizzard, there's a winter wonderland

Twin Lakes Bridge - Mammoth Lakes
oil on canvas, 30 x 24 inches

Silver Lake - June Lake Loop
oil on canvas, 24 x 30 inches

isherman's Tale

Freshly fallen leaves casually floating by
The scene quiets the mind, pleases the eye

Here the pulse slows, the spirit soars
Gently shoving off, you man both oars

Rowing out in your favorite alpine lake
Savoring the reflections quaking aspen make

And even if it isn't trout fishing season
That's not enough of a sportsman's reason

Not to fib about the huge one that got away
Turning your weekend trip into a two-week stay

Surely, your boss would understand the situation
Better still, maybe offer you a permanent vacation

ivin' Large

I suppose I could win the lottery one fine day

Sail the seven seas, bathe in spas, and eat gourmet

I could move here to the hills, build a home to impress

Hire a consultant to choose how I would dress

To the evening ball at my celebrity neighbor's estate

Arriving in my convertible with my head-turning date

Of course, I'd need to schedule a massage the next day

Before the eighteen holes at the country club I'd play . . .

Then again, I'd miss old friends at pizza and beer dinner

Guess I'm just not cut out to be a grand lottery winner

Hollywood Reservoir
oil on canvas, 30 x 24 inches

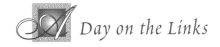 Day on the Links

Out in this scenic valley, we head for the links
To enjoy some camaraderie and 19th-hole drinks

The desert air whips up an early morning haze
I've entered the zone, the golfer's daze
Could this be chronic or is it just another phase?
Am I hopeless or will I shake it one of these days?

Problems of the outside world matter not today
What could be more pressing than this round to play?
I'm on a golfer's high but here I so precariously stay
Then the evil 17th hole—the dragon I can never slay

Alcatraz—they call it—and no less entertaining
Its namesake warrants some simple explaining
A green on and island built for detaining
Criminals like me with little or no golf training

Undaunted, I tee-up and bravely let fly
Ker-plunk, again and again, into water chest high
So my mood crashes and I simply ask why
The 19th hole, now, seems so far to the eye

PGA West - La Quinta
oil on canvas, 32 x 16 inches

Malibu
oil on canvas, 24 x 36 inches

Intertidal Zone

This is how my beachcombing day goes

The ocean's untiring tide ebbs and flows

Cool water at my feet soothes my state of mind

Daydreaming to a dynamic sea foam design

I fantasize of a home on stilts over land's end

Sharing a sunset drink with a good old friend

Or telling stories to grandchildren who beg for another

While I sneak a wink at their amused grandmother

Wouldn't it be nice to call the intertidal zone

The place on which you built your life's dream home

Chapter 3

Reverence, Gratitude, and Respect

Gratitude

Emerald, azure water below

Worries your cool depths drown

Snow flecked mountains afar

I hear your distant call

My adventuresome heart your beckoning crows

Lush forests taunting timberline above

Righteous lust for life your eminence rejuvenates

Pure white clouds in crystal air aloft

I feel the lift of your earth pulling defiance

My pulse quickening dreams your miracle claims possible

Earthly path before me

Intrusion your warmth indiscriminantly welcomes

Solemn giant cloaked in arbor garb on island hither

I absorb the humble message of your peaceful existence

Beneath you I shall sing to all these in purest, sincerest gratitude

Lake Sabrina
oil on canvas, 40 x 30 inches

Beavertail Cactus - Mojave Desert
oil on canvas, 24 x 36 inches

Nature's Happenstance

Unabashedly seductive, beavertail cactus

Beamingly irresistible, indiscreet temptress

By the light of day, offering her sweet nectar

Buzzing takers by the score come greet her

Each reveling in an afternoon delight

Before their next self-indulgent flight

Landing again, they may unwittingly succeed

In delivering cactus pollen to an accepting seed

The birds and bees and nature's simple romances

How beautiful life born of divine happenstances

Ponder if You Can

Suppose no one observes the delicate icicles

Gone forever after tomorrow's thaw?

What if no one witnesses today's cool, blue sky

Reflected in the shadows of this snowy north face?

Imagine for a moment

If everything you created was a miracle

And most were never even seen

And fewer, still, truly appreciated.

Convict Lake
oil on canvas, 30 x 24 inches

American River
oil on canvas, 24 x 36 inches

hy the River Flows

Last night's snow, so pure and pristine

This morning's air, so crisp and clean

Testing the water at a bend in the river

My hand recoils with a chill and a shiver

But forever and again the river flows

From wherever it comes and wherever it goes

On the passing water I let my thoughts glide

Past a wedged log and down a rock slide

From this vantage I know why the river flows

And why the water surges even after wintry snows

Why it rushes to meet the distant sea

And why on rafts it carries you and me

Gravity would be the logical explanation

But I suspect a more impassioned motivation

If the water could speak, this it would say:

How blessed I am to be in the river today

For I've been boiled with noodles, flushed down the drain

Raised to the heavens and hurtled down as rain

Been drunk in a gulp and passed through gills of fishes

Washed the laundry and rinsed the dishes . . .

All these I do with great joy and exultation

For I was His first earthly creation

ave Maker

Beneath the morning desert sky

Waves of sand dunes do please my eye

Seemingly taught by counterpart sea

These waves share the same mystery

Sand and sea, opposed though they may,

Relate to each other in the same way

For nature and all her keen science

Is governed by common Guidance

The same Hand guiding me 'til I die

So the sand dunes do please my eye

Mesquite Sand Dunes - Death Valley National Park
oil on canvas, 36 x 24 inches

Yuba River
oil on canvas, 36 x 24 inches

Humility

Passing flora and fauna

Tween mountains, over falls, down through meadows

Impervious to wind, indifferent to fire

The river—nature's great leadership example

Its journey to greet the sea undeterred

None reigns like the river

And still lays itself deeper below its peers

e, the Fleeting Tenants

Cloaked in morning fog he stands proud

Sunlight shafts surround in pale shroud

Centuries withstanding nature's elements

Largest living thing on seven continents

Amidst this Goliath of all the earth

Neighboring trees bow to his mighty girth

Next to their humility mine seems irrelevant

Beside their heft I am lost and insignificant

When in irreverence man claims Earth his own

These giants suggest we descend our selfish throne

General Sherman Tree - Sequoia National Park
oil on canvas, 24 x 36 inches

Joshua Tree National Park
oil on canvas, 30 x 24 inches

ulnerability

Slowly, increasingly the noises grew

A buzz, a rustle, followed by something shrill

Then a silent, pregnant pause to intensify my unrest

But the cacophony returned and hit a fevered pitch

All invisible, all indecipherable to me

Eerie noises in this alien place

Those once comical trees, now sinister silhouettes

Long shadows, now dissolved into dusk

Today's searing heat, now a chilly memory

Where once the desert was quiet, now it's alive

Where once I was alone, now I am lonely

Once certain, even complacent, of my place in this world

It occurs to me the small fraction of this planet I can tame

How vast and eternal it all seems

Compared to my own fleck of mass and flashing lifetime

I gain a deeper appreciation for this massive, timeless, orbiting rock

Traveling effortlessly, ceaselessly through space

A greater realization of my own vulnerability and minuteness

And an uneasiness in the injustice that, for all our relative insignificance,

It is still we who most jeopardize the planet's own vulnerability

nsurpassed

Inspiring waterfalls in wide variety

Stupendous escarpment so high and mighty

Alpine lakes pristine and crystal clear

Flowering meadows and foraging deer

Skies casting a different drama every day

Four seasons change in spectacular display

A similar place more soulfully enriching

On this planet, I cannot imagine existing

Glacier Point - Yosemite National Park
oil on canvas, 40 x 30 inches

Golden Gate Bridge - San Francisco
oil on canvas, 24 x 36 inches

By No Other Name

Not just cold, riveted steel

An engineering marvel

Not just a practical overpass

A romantic passage

Not just port entry

An open gate

Not just a basic thoroughfare

An aesthetic pleasure

Not just a picture opportunity

A national landmark

No, not just an anonymous bridge

The Golden Gate

il Death Do Us Part

Full throes of autumn, harvest near

Hills recede in sumptuous atmosphere

The great matriarch giving of her fruited land

Loving us, nurturing her children at hand

Dusk paints a monochromatic landscape scene

Limited palette suggesting a harmonious theme

In the shallow distance an old oak tree stands

A patriarch worthy of the respect he commands

A proud symbol of strength and dependability

The raw foundations for safety and stability

Thus, is illustrated holy matrimony so heavenly

Mother Earth and Father Time in perfect harmony

Napa Valley
oil on canvas, 30 x 24 inches

Mono Lake
oil on canvas, 48 x 24 inches

 rossroads

On the eastern edge of the Sierra Nevada range

Lies a peculiar salt lake with towers quite strange

Tufa towers—those eerie mineral formations—

Crumble like gravestones from lost civilizations

Ancient sacred land, this seems to my imagination

Where sagebrush and unsavory water stir contemplation

Of a settler's westward journey and constant threat of doom

For beyond this final signpost, ever more danger would loom

Warning for the westbound of their impending plight

While also a life source for birds in migratory flight

A curious crossroads with an interesting significance

A reminder of the need for our inter-species coexistence

Indeed, the need to remember our delicate interdependence

Lest we be dealt the wrath of the sacred land's vengeance

enaissance

Our dizzying progress, always progress

Hither and forth, then back again but always going

Onward, ho!

The path endless, beckoning still further

Further the engine chugs, absent a prescribed destination

Generations bounding ahead faster, knowing not wherefore

The desert has no use for such progress

Here there is no elusive destination, only the process—

To be born, to live, to expire, to begin anew

Perennial miracles, the glory of the daily hum-drum

Ingenious the creativity to beget against extreme odds

And if our engine of progress, God forbid, chugs along too far an errant rail

Puffing so blindly no earthly force may ebb its momentum

Genius resurrector, battle-tough and tested, hold strong

For if Grace were to give us another chance

In you I have faith to cradle life anew

Red Rock Canyon
oil on canvas, 24 x 36 inches

Chapter 4

Absorbing Her Lessons

Morro Bay
oil on canvas, 24 x 36 inches

eachcombing for Dollars

Combing the beach, sand dollars strewn

Some large, some small

Some white, some yellowed

But each one broken

Nary a dollar whole, each broken in its own way

Some chipped, some halved, some without top

On I sought, collecting remnants along

More resolute I grew. I shall find one whole!

A dog chasing gulls my concentration broke

The silly fool. He'll never catch one

Egad! What if someone watching me would say the same

Like the dog's futile hunt

So my quest for the sand dollar

So, too, my appetite for wealth

Repentantly, the sand dollar remnants along the shore I flung

How beautiful they looked strewn across the wet sand

I savored my beachcombing stroll

The cackle of the gulls, the late afternoon sun, the sea spray

The joy of the dog's game and indifference to winning his prize

The gentle rise of a spent wave lapping at my feet

And in its retreat, a whole sand dollar unveiled

and of Riches

It was here James Marshall found a famous, gold nugget

Starting a rush of those who panned and dug for it

They sailed across oceans and trekked over continents

Fueled by hope and sometimes foolish confidence

They came in search of wealth in limitless extremes

But most were dealt lessons in greed and broken dreams

But who could fault them for such enterprising adventure

And who at the time would even dare to conjecture

That from these efforts a foundation would be laid

Upon which our great "Golden State" would be made

That is to say, a different type of wealth was found

Where beauty, natural riches, and ingenuity abound

Sutter's Mill - South Fork of the American River
oil on canvas, 32 x 16 inches

Emerald Bay - Lake Tahoe
oil on canvas, 24 x 36 inches

Independent Thinker

As if a herd of like-minded sheep

The geese an orderly flock do keep

But today I saw one set astray

Indeed, journey off on his own way!

He was drawn by the snow's reflection

And alluring opening in that same direction

I read his mind while he looked back—

"Follow my path or stick with the pack?"

Courageously he carried on with ambition

Using blind faith and his sense of intuition

If a goose could follow what others can't see

Then for heaven's sake, why not you and me?

The Precious Moment

Reading an ancient canyon like history's pages

I wonder how man survived through the ages

As for my own past, where has it brought me?

If not for this or that, oh. . . where I would be!

The rising sun reminds me of my day ahead

And all I must do before I lay myself to bed

And the day after that and the next tomorrow

Where will it all lead? What will follow?

Then my anxiety suffers a momentary lapse

As my useless worries suddenly collapse

Soaking in that which before me I see

A foreign inner peace descends upon me

Don't fret of the future nor live in the past

Revel in the moment as if it's your last

King's Canyon National Park
oil on canvas, 36 x 24 inches

Point Lobos State Reserve
oil on canvas, 36 x 24 inches

# Remembering

At this magnificent meeting of land and sea I am reminded

Reminded, that is,

      Of the rejuvenating power of wandering on uneven land

      The life-giving energy of breathing the air of tall trees

      The refreshing calm of catching an on-shore breeze

      The therapeutic rhythms of wading among undulating waves

      The cathartic release of listening to crashing surf

Here, I cannot help but wonder

Wonder, that is, if our ever more metropolitan humanity

Will, like me, be ever more likely to forget such things

ountain of Knowledge

A two-tiered fountain trickles water in a lily pond

Mission facade brightly mirrored, cobalt background

Something about the wavy reflection before me

Stirs daydreams of the mission's history

I imagine people's lives quite different from mine

And that's not far back along history's time line

I can't help but wonder a few centuries hence

How we'll be living and how we'll dispense

Of current problems and how prosperous we'll be

Where it will all lead and what our eyes will see

So, I ask the fountain for answers to my questions

But she just carries on offering no suggestions

She's unperturbed by the goings on around her

Never tiring of the next tourist encounter

She simply trickles on at her own gentle pace

At peace with her purpose to beautify this place

In the flow of her trickle, I get her clue

And understand her serene, simple point of view

Focus only on things within your influential scope

Accept everything else with loving faith and hope

Santa Barbara Mission
oil on canvas, 30 x 24 inches

La Jolla
oil on canvas, 36 x 36 inches

Rock in the Cove

Blooming ice plant the cliff top covers

Near a sheltered overlook fit for lovers

From their vantage, there's much to adore

Arm in arm, sound of waves lapping ashore

A pelican hits the water in dive-bomb formation

While sea lions frolic as if on summer vacation

In the cove carved by waves down below

A rock is putting on an impressive show

Succumbing not to erosion, strong and steadfast

Lovers ponder if their love will likewise last

Will it crash the way the pelican dove

Or will it be robust like the rock in the cove?

abbling Brook

Where not many months ago

The mountain teemed with bountiful life

Balmy skies and daylight ever longer

Slowly, green turned auburn, gold, then brown

Harbingers of death's hand, so slow and deliberate

Balmy went chilly, cold, then freezing

Old Man Winter reeking his wrath, seemingly unrelenting

Eventually he released his grip, though not willfully

Stubbornly melting into silent drops

But each contributing to the brook's whispering trickle

Patiently, each day a little more before at long last

Green in reprise as daylight grew longer

And the brook babbled in giddy celebration

To each beginning, an end

To each end, a new beginning

Lassen Volcanic National Park
oil on canvas, 24 x 30 inches

Pismo Beach
oil on canvas, 30 x 24 inches

 *hoppy surf*

In shallow, choppy surf his best effort he gave

Making great show of a poor surfing wave

As with our own lives, I've come to understand

We've been given free will and dealt a certain hand

What we do with each hand is of our own choosing

Whether we see things as bad luck or opportunity brewing

True, conditions around us we can't control or dictate

But, as with the surfer, it's attitude which most defines fate

dversity

Stark vibe pervades the atmosphere

Man nor beast dares reside here

Inhospitable this grim aura

Rude to all fauna and flora

One hero, nevertheless, survives

Moreover, it is here where he thrives

Sweet are adversity's uses

Which bore this child of such abuses

Could our troubles have utility?

Could a tree dismiss futility?

Bristlecone Pine - White Mountains
oil on canvas, 36 x 24 inches

Lake Shastina
oil on canvas, 36 x 24 inches

f Things to Come

How tranquil this placid landscape

Ah, but these mountains borne of upheaval

A burning caldron arisen

    Made to cool and petrify

How glorious these brilliant sun beams

The promising serenity of things to come

Made possible by the once fierce storm

    Now passing so peacefully by

So it is I see a clear parallel

Our clouds, too, have silver linings

Implausible to us while weathering the storm

    But just waiting for the right time to shine

Living on the Edge

The sharp edged line of light and dark

Traversed so precariously every day

To discern the shadowy abyss from goodness

I can only seek my Source and pray

That I might see clearly as black and white

Instead so many shades of gray

If only white were always good

And black led only astray

I'd paint a white picture and call it

"This is the only way!"

Broken Hill - Torrey Pines State Reserve
oil on canvas, 24 x 36 inches

Sonoma Valley
oil on canvas, 24 x 36 inches

As You Sow, So Shall You Reap

Impossible it would be for a rotten grape vine

To bear succulent fruit

Or a decrepit rose bush

To bring forth a brilliant flower

If only I could follow this vintner's enviable example . . .

If only I could nurture my body and soul

As the farmer his beloved land

How vivacious and vibrant I might one day become

Solidarity

Architectural marvel of Michelangelo creation—

The rotunda, emblematic of democratic civilization

Its likeness found throughout our great nation

Flattery to the artist in the form of imitation

Marvelously robust with each piece firmly situated

Perilously fragile when even one is eliminated

The participation of each piece necessary but equal

As with democracy and each of its people

State Capitol Building - Sacramento
oil on canvas, 24 x 36 inches

Mt. Whitney as seen from the Alabama Hills
oil on canvas, 36 x 24 inches

Glowing Bounty for an Early Riser

I rise early for this my favorite show

Nature's great spectacle, the alpenglow

Yesterday's craggy peaks of granite gray

Ablaze in the colors of the dawning day

Violet, crimson, orange then gold

Light's awesome spectrum, big and bold

As I watch in rapt fascination

I wish to suspend the animation

Why so fleeting its glorious stay?

I wish it could last the entire day

But then I'd lose the dumb fascination

It's true—all good things in moderation

ot Head

Upon my arrival, it hid from my sight

Its base barely visible in overcast twilight

But there it was this morning when I awoke

Whisked away was its massive, cloudy cloak

The sun rising at dawn's deliberate pace

Casting shadows on its long, sloping face

Standing on an island surrounded by a lake

A place virtually made for a picture's sake

A cool fog burned off the lake's mirrored surface

Oh, the unrest once stirring in Shasta's furnace

Which, deep down, not many years ago

Caused its massive top to suddenly blow

Spewing streams of molten lava down below

And scattering ashes like fresh, December snow

It is said, many a secret the mountains keep

Not unlike my stress under the rug I sweep

Perhaps, if a habit of this I continue to make

My top, too, will suffer the same fate

Mt. Shasta as seen from Lake Shastina
oil on canvas, 24 x 30 inches

Bodie State Historic Park
oil on canvas, 24 x 24 inches

Farewell

At the end of my road

It'll matter . . .

Not how polished my appearance

But rather how strong my integrity

Not how I died

But rather how I lived

Not how I'm remembered

But rather how my legacy lives on

Chapter 5

Discovering Silence, Dreaming, and Believing

Lone Cypress - Pebble Beach
oil on canvas, 20 x 24 inches

 *onundrum of the Lone Cypress*

The peaceful embrace of solitude

And the stark beauty found in silence

Is, I fear, an inexhaustible challenge

Not easily mastered in a lifetime

But, a lifetime spent

Not exhausting oneself in the challenge

Is, I suspect, a life not aptly mastered

heatre of the Soul

Front row seats to the show at river's edge

Torrents of water falling off a rocky ledge

Thunderous streams cascade down the middle

While from the face, gentle flows slowly dribble

A refreshing mist caresses my weathered face

Closing my eyes, I return a loving embrace

In this way, I allow myself to feel more acutely

And take in the surroundings more absolutely

In the fullness of this invigorating meditation

All ambient energy pumps through my circulation

My body returns the energy with a tingling vibration

I feel in perfect harmony with the spirit of creation

Grateful am I for seats in this magnificent theatre

Times like these, I feel closest to the Divine Creator

McArthur-Burney Falls Memorial State Park
oil on canvas, 40 x 30 inches

Anza-Borrego Desert State Park
oil on canvas, 36 x 24 inches

Til Only My Spirit Remains

You of forsaken landscapes

You do not know the footprint in the sand of a summer beach

Nor the stream of an alpine meadow

You have never known the nourishing yield of a fertile field

Never the shade of an old oak tree

You do not know these, for I know them and I know not you

No. . . I know not you

Why then do you intrigue me so?

Amidst your imposing power I realize my precarious mortality

Your parched silence my layers peel 'til only my core remains

Great masters seeking truth have ventured to you in solitude

But alone with you, I know not the tenderness of a loving hand

Not the fruited plain, not the roof over my home

Stripped of everything 'til only my spirit remains

My opinions useless, and others of me sillier yet

No noise for me to filter, no need for me to speak

I know not you but, alas

Thanks to you, now, I know myself

athedral Hush

Brilliant rhododendron in bloom, so delicate and seemingly naive

Strikingly juxtaposed before a fallen redwood, once so mighty and seemingly wise

Beneath this cavernous canopy

One can smell the perfume of life

The rotting decay of death

Indeed their interconnectedness

In this deafening silence, my most fundamental, biological core

Finds spiritual kinship with the pervasive organic energy

One senses the work of a divine hand, patiently creating from ash and dust

Looking up through a small hole in the cover, I reverently whisper

"Sweet, resplendent cathedral hush. . . how glorious thou art!"

Jedediah Smith Redwoods State Park
oil on canvas, 24 x 36 inches

Natural Bridges State Beach - Santa Cruz
oil on canvas, 30 x 24 inches

Tunnel Vision

It's one of those days of inescapable stress

Anxiety, tension and choice under duress

Whereto has my energy drained?

Why is my mind so scatter-brained?

To silence the cacophony stirring in my mind

A sanctuary I envision where I escape from the grind

It takes the shape of a shoreline rock formation

With a hole in the middle to center my concentration

Through its dark tunnel I'm drawn to the bright sea

Here, in sharp focus I channel positive energy

Problems shielded out, rock solid and sound

In this contemplative state, solutions abound

For here I discern what my heart yearns to say—

"Relax, have faith, your anxieties you shall slay"

And so, I dispatch shorebirds like bombardiers

One for each pesky demon and all my silly fears

llumination

The little boy grew up in search of knowledge.
He listened to what his parents said, what other wise people said.

The boy went to school, more knowledge he sought.
He listened to the teachers, more information they uncorked.

Then someone gave him important direction.
There is power in mastering specific information.
So, he prostrated to the higher minds of higher education.
Absorbed volumes of science, history, economics, philosophy.
Dissected his own language and learned tongues of far nations.
Finally, the graduate stood steeped in information.

Long gone the little boy who had sought knowledge.
Now a grown man empowered with information, decades of it.
Real world information kept coming in inconquerable waves.
More data, more stimulus, more noise.

A faint voice grew louder. More silence, solitude, even darkness it demanded.
The man planned to sneak away someday.
Indulge in the forbidden wishes of the voice.
He planned it well with all his information.
He chose a desolate place in the dead of night.
Like the liberating pleasure of screaming naked from a mountaintop,
Here, in a crazy fit, he simply let it all go.

In a moment of clarity he realized the information had been helpful but incomplete:

    It had been the menu, not the food

    The rules of the game, not the sport

    The map, not the journey

The little boy's curiosity and thirst for experience returned.

His appetite for the simple beauty in life rediscovered.

His inner voice heard. Knowledge at last.

Zabriskie Point - Death Valley National Park
oil on canvas, 32 x 16 inches

Mendocino Headlands State Park
oil on canvas, 36 x 24 inches

# Headland Romance

Walking a trail past dewy seathrift

Down to the beach, mind set adrift

We throw off our shoes dismissing concern and care

Taking in the headland scenery and fresh ocean air

We behold the sea forever faithfully greeting land

Leaving two pairs of footprints in the cool, shoreline sand

How blessed we are to enjoy such a place together

I pray we may share such simple grace forever

he Answer's in the Stars

In a fresh spring meadow I stand amidst a patch of blooming shooting stars.

The miracle of Nature's engineering drives my bewilderment.

From where this ability for these plants to grow and know exactly when?

My mind goes numb thinking of all the earth's living matter

And even the atomic structure of things inorganic, for that matter,

The interconnectedness of life and its masterful balance

The weather, the seasons, even earth's gravity and atmosphere.

And as for the stars above,

For each I can count, it is said,

There are at least as many galaxies! And within each, who can tell?

Ponder a universe infinite and ever expanding,

Random and chaotic but yet somehow masterfully designed.

As for the answers to such mysteries,

I need look no further than right here.

No further than beyond these blooming shooting stars

For in the Grace bestowed upon each, my faith is renewed.

Tuolomne Meadows - Yosemite National Park
oil on canvas, 36 x 24 inches

 ailing Away

Remembering late, loved ones and where they've gone
Their love eternal as the ocean's murmuring song

Sailing quietly and carefree but not aimlessly
Navigating the placid course of destiny
On the horizon, an island stirs the imagination
Of a still more idyllic and peaceful destination

Mysterious clouds painting improbable patterns above
Seemingly heaven-sent on the wings of an artful dove
Only faith provides answers to life hereafter
But, for now, it's as clear as the gulls cackling laughter

Because, you see, you must focus on the here and now
Your busy mind is required for its savvy know-how
For in front of you an earthly path turns a bend
And you know not what to expect or on whom to depend

In this marvelous vista you detect some spiritual clues
But is your heart open enough in faith to choose?

Corona del Mar - Orange County
oil on canvas, 24 x 36 inches

Sunset Rendezvous

Later that day you return to the same location
Drawn by the day's earlier contemplation

You've been agonizing over this throughout the day
In a spiritual moment, the words come and so you pray...

One day our wind will wane, our sun will set
Nothing we can do but no need to fret
Yes, sadly, loved ones will be left behind
But coming home is our reward in due time
For some day when our work is done, we, too, will follow
Oh, the beautiful sunset rendezvous of that fateful tomorrow!

Corona del Mar - Orange County
oil on canvas, 20 x 16 inches

Guardian Angel

There have been times . . .

A rose has looked at me more lovingly than I beheld its beauty

A song has known me better than I knew its lyrics

A waft of air has consumed me more than I inhaled it.

There have been times

I have wandered far in safety, though I knew not the way.

Carmel Mission
oil on canvas, 24 x 30 inches

Trinidad
oil on canvas, 48 x 24 inches

Legend of Chief Sitting Sunset

Strange sea stacks perched like monuments to history

Vaguely reminiscent of the famous Stonehenge mystery

As if I didn't find this place fascinating enough

I see an Indian from my vantage on this bluff

Actually a likeness of his profile, old and wise

Carved in rock on the nearest stack's far rise

Stoically he gazes, each day, out over ocean sunsets

Content with his calling, sitting silently, no regrets

"Chief Sitting Sunset" I playfully call him by name

Forever planted, each day's routine just the same

I guess it doesn't matter what one's true obsession

Even if its being a sunset watcher by profession

In being true to the calling whatever it may be

The heart must feel before the imagination can see

And when one sees clearly with the Chief's honest eyes

Only then will one's true calling materialize

# Mount up with Strength Like Eagles

The respect we all have for this magnificent thing

His freedom, his grace, his position as king

But there's a side of him even more alluring to me

Than being so powerful and being so free

From hatchling on, a raptor he knows he must be

By contrast how difficult our purpose is to see

That reminds me of a fable I once was told

Of an eagle raised by chickens, conforming to their mold

The eagle grew up not knowing how to fly

When, one day he saw one soaring up high

He stood silent for a moment in contemplation

Then to his chicken friends, made a bold declaration

If given a choice to be something else instead

I'd be a mighty eagle flying high overhead

So it is that your own remarkable life's course

May lie concealed within a deep inner source

Listen to these rumblings, lend them true vitality

And before long your dreams will become reality

Twin Lakes
oil on canvas, 24 x 36 inches

American and California Flags at Sunset
oil on canvas, 24 x 36 inches

Gallantly Gleaming

Banner of this great state 'neath Stars and Stripes

Prancing gracefully in tandem

To the whims of a twilight breeze

The setting sun ignites the duo with a gilded glow

Telling the story of the American dream

And the lure of California gold

The mind wanders to those who came before

What they have made

And how we their lead might follow

Like the whims of the twilight breeze

So, too, the uncertain future

But like the strength of the bear

Our faith and resolve shall be

To achieve an ever more perfect republic

Chapter 6

Queen Califia Concludes

Eureka!

The hills an opera began to perform
Before my eyes my heart they did warm
First, they sang of prospector dreams
Forty-niners panning gold rush streams
Then they sang of subsequent generations—
More dream seekers of near and far nations

A stirring aria the poppy chorus wailed
Of a magical place the world over hailed
Regaled for its unique free spiritedness
And cornucopia of opportunity endless

Down a trail, the lupines' tenor ushered
At every turn more loving beauty I discovered
Color bursts sent me into visual delirium
One-hundred fifty years at the new millennium!

In my daze I failed to comprehend
The big picture on the path with no end
With the crescendo of a kettle drum rumble
Storm clouds tripped my skip to a stumble
"Look up here," they demandingly bellowed
Their tone my mood instantly mellowed

The namesake of California in epiphany came—
Queen Califia was her nobly respected name
A striking protagonist made of sun and rain
A half-rainbow with a glorious soprano strain

She sang of heaven on earth within our grasp
If only the antagonist would allow it to pass
In falsetto she revealed passions and fears
With melancholy so pure, clouds poured tears

Then came silence as storm clouds cleared
It couldn't be over. No antagonist had appeared
The silence continued, my discomfort grew
Don't leave me hanging. What should I do?

No answer came so in the silence I spoke,
"What is this folly? I don't get your silly joke
Your vision of heaven on earth seems out of focus
How could this ever happen? It's all hocus pocus!"

Still no answer came. How long could this last?
As my anger mounted, my scripted roll was cast
Suddenly I realized I was the source of her concern
Surprise! I was the antagonist in this tragic turn
"Me! Why me? What did I do for this to deserve?"
"Why hold me responsible? You've got your nerve!"

She had me. Played me like a grand piano
Then she cut loose in her beautiful soprano:

> *Not just you, this is important for all to know*
> *Everyone must help complete my full rainbow*
> *Take to heart what my friends to you have sung*
> *A message of love and harmony not far-flung*
> *If humanity could follow Nature's honest lead*
> *Indeed a heaven could here on earth succeed*
> *With each kind act done or hateful one defeated*
> *Another piece of my rainbow will be completed*
> *On the state's anniversary of a century and a half*
> *Celebrate the distance you've come down the path*
> *But as you begin millennium number three*
> *Know there's much work to reach the destiny*
> *There is hope for the miracle to begin anywhere*
> *But as for me, my mission is to start right here*
> *The fountain of your soul you must tap*
> *This is the Truth—your life's road map*
> *Do good things with your talent and skill*
> *These are God's gifts. My rainbow you will fill!*
> *As we have sung to you, shall you to others sing*
> *In so doing a great millennium you all will bring*

An inspirational surge welled up inside my heart
This great state my soul sought from the start
I reflected on the California state seal
Eureka! it proclaims with a discoverer's zeal
On this birthday and millennium begun anew
I, too, shouted "Eureka!" painting a hill top view

California Poppy Reserve - Antelope Valley
oil on canvas, 30 x 40 inches

This California tableau was a humble attempt to do justice to an extraordinarily diverse state. The paintings reproduced in this book were created from inspirations of a dozen different trips, totalling about 15,000 miles of travel. Although I embarked upon these excursions with a loose plan of what I wanted to see, I did, nevertheless, allow myself the latitude to be inspired by whatever I stumbled upon. During the trips, I amassed a large collection of photographs while tape recording notes on the ambience of each place. Upon seeing places which I was certain I would paint, I took time to meditate on the spot. Each meditation was an effort to connect with the scene and its ambience but also a prayer that I might do justice to the real life beauty I was beholding. These meditations brought life to my photos and audible notes while infusing my creativity with passion.

The poems were in some instances inspired by observations made and ideas gleaned on location. For the most part, however, each poem was composed after the respective painting was completed. Thus, most of the poems were borne of the meanderings of my mind while creating the paintings.

In my writing verse to accompany each piece, I hoped the reader would achieve a stronger connection with the essence of the composition. Moreover, I wanted to tell a story of the complete odyssey—one not plainly rooted in the physical but also in the emotional and spiritual.

To be sure *California: Through An Artist's Eye* is just that—a place seen through only one pair of eyes. My observations are infused with my own experiences and ideas. Therein, however, lies the beauty of personal observation and expression. For me, and I suppose for most, beholding inspiring landscapes creates a contemplative state of mind which allows us to get in touch with our deepest thoughts. It is a simple pleasure which, I fear, has become ever more difficult to practice in our increasingly fast-paced lives.

I feel extremely fortunate to pursue this as my livelihood, to have been granted the gift of art, and to have the freedom to express it. I feel likewise grateful to have been in the position to undertake this particular collection. It has been an especially wonderful and gratifying journey of an extraordinary place. Long may this great state touch the human spirit.

Oil painting is a profoundly fulfilling experience for me. It is about the enjoyment of immersing myself in a process for which I am passionate. Above all, oil painting to me is about a feeling of having discovered a sense of purpose.

In previous occupations, while pursuing "more practical" livelihoods, something seemed to be missing, even in the face of apparent outward successes. Slowly, I realized I was ignoring something more personally important, something far more exciting.

When the artist finally emerged, he did so loudly—with intense color. This use of high chroma in my paintings is a reflection of my spirit's adulation of pursuing its real passion. The realistic painting style I employ is an outcropping of my engineering background and respect for detail and logical order. "Landscape and Lifestyle" is the loose term I give my subject matter which finds its roots in my penchant for travel. The resulting amalgamation of all these elements defines my painting style.

I have tried to explore different painting styles, but never with any feeling of authenticity. Also, perhaps due to my lack of formal art training, I have not been exposed to instructive influences, for better or worse. As a result, I like to think my true personality is reflected in my painting.

Similarly, the verse I write to accompany each piece is not something which has been taught. It is simple and raw. It is not the style, however, which I intend to impress upon the beholder but rather a profound sense of what my heart sees and feels.

Pursuing a passion is a spiritual journey. Indeed passions cannot be directed without addressing some sort of spiritual compass. In choosing the mediums of oil painting and verse to communicate that about which I am passionate, a deeper sense of my spirit has been revealed. This in turn has stirred deeper creative juices. So it is how, I believe, my creativity grows and evolves.

Over time, I can only wonder how my painting and writing styles will evolve, from where the sources of my inspiration will come, or to where they will take me. *How fascinating it is to explore the intriguing journey of one's own creative spirit!*

Previous Titles by Steve Simon

Newport Beach, California
112 pages, 11 x 8-1/2 inches

Steve Simon's first bound collection of work includes forty-six scenes of Newport Beach, California, locations and includes the artist's comments on historical and anecdotal points of interest.

Retail Price: $34.95

Orange County: Through An Artist's Eye
112 pages, 8-1/2 x 11 inches

Steve Simon's second bound collection of work includes fifty-five scenes of Orange County, California, scenes. Each image is accompanied by the artist's rhyming verse.

Retail Price: $34.95

Purchasing Art

To request a price list of reproductions of the images found in this publication, please contact the *Simon Fine Art Gallery & Studio* or the artist's website. Contact information is provided below. A variety of Steve Simon lithographs, giclée prints, calendars, greeting cards, and other items are available.

Simon Fine Art Gallery & Studio

Simon Fine Art Gallery & Studio serves as the artist's flagship gallery and working studio. It is located on friendly Balboa Island in the seaside community of Newport Beach, California.

Simon Fine Art Gallery & Studio
216 Marine Avenue
Balboa Island, CA 92662

Call Toll Free: **1-877-4CA-SCENES**
4 2 2 - 7 2 3 6

Phone: 949-723-1100 • Facsimile: 949-723-1650

www.stevesimon.com

List of Plates